Gratitude

with

The Law of Attraction

Workbook

Gratitude with the Law of Attraction
Workbook

Cover by: Petya Petkova / www.petkomotiv.dk
Edited by: Thomas Rambusch
Proof reading: Bette Cooper
Photo of Bettina Møller Jensen on the cover:
Calin Strajescu / www.instagram.com/calin.photography

Printed at BOD, Germany in 2020

Published by: Books on Demand – Copenhagen, Denmark
1st edition, 1st impression
ISBN: 9788743013891

www.bettinamollerjensen.com
Focus & Flow – The Danish School of deliberate use of the Law of Attraction by Bettina Møller Jensen

FSC
www.fsc.org

MIX

Papir fra
ansvarlige kilder
Paper from
responsible sources

FSC® C105338

You create the magic in your own life.

Grab your magic wand and start today.

Contents

Introduction

In October 2018, I started (another) group on Facebook. This time, the scope of the group was gratitude. For years, I had myself incorporated a daily discipline of gratitude in my own day-to-day life. In correlation with my work with the Law of Attraction, I wanted to spread the word about the significant role of daily gratitude to a broader audience. My intention for the group on Facebook, which is free to participate in, was to show others the tremendous force that lies within the capability to control your focus. When it comes down to learning and implementing new habits in our lives, it is always helpful when you can use a template to build a new routine, so that you just need to do what you are told without paying too much attention to it. The new tracks in your brain will form quicker when you don't have any resistance to the change. As I write this book, the group on Facebook has now existed for more than 14 months since I started the challenge, and every day I feel so much joy when I see the progress in the group. There is a huge gift in the act of gratitude. Gratitude softens your heart. I know that for a fact, because I have been and still am practicing a daily habit of gratitude. Scientists have also told us about the positive benefits of gratitude. Even public persona and celebrities have had their say. You can find posts of gratitude all over various social media platforms.

It is so great to see this trend, because gratitude is a very significant part of being successful when it comes to applying the Law of Attraction deliberately in your life. Initially, the group on Facebook was just a one-week challenge, but people were so enthusiastic about it, the group has now become permanent and counts close to a thousand participants who share their gratitude daily. The act of gratitude helps to raise the vibes and the energy, not only for the ones sharing their gratitude posts, but also for the ones reading them.

So, why is this workbook necessary?

As the only Certified Law of Attraction Facilitator in Denmark, I work with energy and vibes every day, and often I meet people who find it difficult to change their habits and to stick to them over time.

If you are into yoga or interested in the yoga world, you might have heard the term: *tapas*.

Of course, *tapas* could be delicious, little dishes to be enjoyed by candlelight while writing your daily gratitude. In this case, it is something completely different. In the yoga world, *tapas* means heat, and symbolizes the action that happens when we burn off residues of karma or bad habits. Thus, *tapas* is the self-discipline to be able to dedicate yourself to a practice that serves the purpose of you yourself being the fire and the force that produces and ignites the transformation and change. A *tapas* is not a mechanical repetition, instead a *tapas* is conducted with attention, determination and intention.

A *tapas* can vary in length. In this case, the *tapas* is 108 days. 108 is the figure for spiritual completeness and is seen in other areas. Among others, 108 is the number of beads in a Mala. In yoga, the Sun Salutation consists of nine parts that are repeated 12 times, in total 108. 108 is also the number of energy lines in our systems and, of course, 108 is also the number of repetitions of the mantra Shreem Brzee.

You can choose to follow the 108-day *tapas* in this book, or you can choose something else that fits better with your life.

On the following pages, you will find an inspirational list you can use if you find it difficult to start your practice of gratitude. Also, you will find a page that shows you examples of how to use this book.

Inspirational list

- My life
- Today
- Me
- My relations
- The country I live in
- The city I live in
- The place I live
- Nature
- Earth
- Fauna
- Flora
- Food I have tasted
- Experiences I have had
- Things I have learned
- Places I have been
- People that have played a significant part in my life
- My body
- Music

Example: How to do this

When you write your daily gratitude, it is important that you describe WHAT you are grateful for and WHY you are grateful for exactly that. When you describe the 'why', you activate the feelings that are attached to what you are grateful for.

Use the examples below for inspiration:

I am grateful for another day, because that means I'm still alive.

I am grateful for the place I live, because I feel safe.

I am grateful for the nature around us, because it always shifts my mood and makes me calm, when I go there.

I am grateful for my sister, because she always has my back and she is there for me, whenever I need her.

I am grateful for my bed, because it gives me a place to rest.

What you focus on expands

You attract what you spend
the most time on

Watch your words

It has to feel good

Your feelings are always telling the truth

_____

Trust your intuition

If it feels bad, it often is

Trust your feelings

Your vibration is gradually rising

The Law of Attraction reflects your

vibration back to you

_____

The better it is, the better it becomes

Reset your vibe by moving your focus

Adventure awaits

_____

Give your burden away

Pay attention to your words

Do you focus more on what you want or what you do not want?

_____

If you want something to go away, stop

giving it your attention

Speak more about what you want

_____

Write about things you like

Talk less about what you do not want

_____

What you give attention to, you give your energy to

What you speak about, you give your energy to

_____

Just because you cannot see it does not mean that it doesn't exist

---

The Law of Attraction works whether you believe it or not

Your focus creates your reality

Spend time doing what you like

What you emit, you attract more of

_____

What you focus on gets stronger

The more time you spend being occupied with something, the more energy you give to it

---

Speak about what you want

The manifestation will come to you with the same intensity as the energy you have given to it

_____

What you are most involved in is also what you invite into your own vibration

_____

Everything starts with your words

_____

Every change starts with you

_____

Your vibration is the essence of what you have been most involved in energetically

_____

What you worry about, you nurture

What you dwell upon in your consciousness

will show up in your reality

Your personality is your reality

Give attention to whatever feels good

_____

Give less attention to what you
do not want

---

*Only say things about yourself that you
want to manifest*

_____

Your feelings are always real

What do you give your attention to?

_____

The energy follows your thoughts

How does it feel?

_____

It has to feel good

Everything is energy

You get a result that is a perfect match
to what you have been most focused on –
whether you like it or not

_____

*Everything you have in your life is a result of
what you have given the most attention to*

There are always at least three solutions to a problem

_____

You have all the resources you need

_____

If you can think the thought,

you can live the thought!

You attract a similar result to what you feel about what you think

---

The Law of Attraction does not care what you focus on, the Law of Attraction merely reflects your vibration back to you

---

You are a living magnet

Take control of your focus and of your behavior

Your future is created from what you do today – not tomorrow!

You create your future this very minute

———————————————————————

Make sure you feel as good as possible

_____

You cannot create anything new from what has happened in the past

---

Worrying is an investment in everything you do not want

The only way to be more positive is by being less negative

Speak more about what you like and less about what you do not like

---

Be brave enough to let go of
what feels wrong

Pay attention to the nuggets

Speak about what you have instead of what
is missing

There is plenty for everybody

_____

Other people do not drag you down. You
choose to lower your own vibration

_____

When something goes wrong, you don't have to go with it

Keep your focus on what works

You see the world from

your own perspective

Other people are merely matching your vibrational expectation

---

Spend more time with people
that fan your flame

Spend less time with people

who dim your light

Miracles tend to happen to people who believe in them

Everything consists of what you choose and what you do not choose

---

Love the contrast. Contrast gives you clarity

You do not have to hang out with people
who affect you negatively

_____

You choose whether you want to send a

positive or a negative vibe

Every single moment you get to choose what you want to focus on. On what you want or what you do not want

_____

You get to choose what you want to give your attention to

Others do not decide what you focus on –

You do

———————————————————

Every moment you are free to choose

another vibe

Be conscious about where you

have your focus

Take control of your thoughts by taking control of your focus

---

If you want another result, you have to change your energy

_____

If you want to know what vibe you are sending, look at your results

---

If you attract the same results again and again, it's because you keep sending the same vibe

---

There are no mistakes. There are only

matches to your vibration

As long as you keep sending the same vibration, you will keep attracting the same results

---

If you got the result, you also sent the vibration

If you do not like it, stop giving your attention to it

When you take control of your focus, you take control of your results

---

The only thing you need to know is what you want

Your feelings are like your GPS, always telling you whether you are on the right track or not

_____

Your desire must be clear for you to attract it

First, you have to know what you want

_____

Compassion for other living beings

releases resistance

Always be kind to others. You never know what their struggle is

---

Your vibration is always a direct reflection of what you are most attracted to

———————————————————

You feel all the time. Therefore, you create
your reality all the time

Whatever you nurture and feed grows

Keep others in the light you want to see them in

_____

You create your own reality

through your feelings

The feeling is important

You create the next moment based upon
how you feel right now

_____

Every thought you have is escorted by a feeling

Your vibration is the true magnet that determines what you attract

---

About Bettina Møller Jensen

Bettina Møller Jensen is a Law of Attraction and Vision Board expert.

Originally, Bettina is a trained and certified Translator and Interpreter in English. For many years before changing her life's course, Bettina worked in the financial sector in various roles.

Today, Bettina uses her skills to help others obtain more freedom and empowerment in their lives by learning how to master the science of deliberate attraction. Bettina uses a variety of modalities such as 1:1 coaching, teaching, and how-to training seminars.

Bettina knows whereof she speaks when it comes to the Law of Attraction. Bettina was trained personally by the internationally renowned Law of Attraction Guru, Michael Losier.

As the only Certified Law of Attraction Facilitator in Denmark, Bettina is known as the go-to Law of Attraction gal and is sometimes referred to as: "The Danish LoA Queen."

Resources

If you want to learn more about the Law of Attraction, please visit our website: www.bettinamollerjensen.com or join my Facebook group: *"Gratitude with the Law of Attraction and Bettina M. Jensen"* for your daily dose of gratitude. On the website you will find a direct link for the group. Or you can follow us on: Instagram.com/bettina.moeller.jensen.